Our World Through My Eyes

My Eyes

A Collection of Children's Poetry

Contents

At Grandma's House

At Grandma's house, I have so much fun.

I can run, and play, and soak in the sun.

At Nana's house, there are good things to eat.

Cookies, pies, ice cream, and other yummy treats.

At Grammy's house, I get lots of hugs.

She treats me so special,

There's nothing like Grammy's love.

At Granny's house, I get lots of cool toys.

She spoils me with fun things that bring me so much joy.

At MaMa's house, I get to stay up late,

Watch movies, eat junk food, and help MaMa bake.

Grandma loves for me to visit.

And I know that whenever I do,

It's my home away from home, and she feels that way too.

Bad Teacher

Assisted by: Liera and Christopher Hairston

Here is a story about one horrible year,

With one horrible teacher, who brought horrible fear.

She did terrible things, unthinkable acts.

She was disgusting, obnoxious and these are the facts!

She yelled for no reason, just for the fright.

She wore all black, the color of midnight.

"Go see the principal!" She yelled, for no reason at all.

We never went outside to play, and when we laughed we had to face the wall.

Who farts and never fesses? This horrible teacher did.

She had dirty, long fingernails, and smelled of a pig.

Halloween was year 'round in this teacher's class.

No pens, no books, but dirty zombie looks.

"I want a new teacher," I begged mom and dad.

"Hang in there, be patient," they said.

Then one day out of nowhere, a new teacher showed up.

The bad teacher was gone, thanks to my good luck.

My new teacher was great! She was everything I wanted.

Learning was fun! We played and we danced, and enjoyed every moment.

Somehow this new teacher managed to relieve my fear,

And repair the damage caused by that horrible, bad teacher that year.

Big Brother, Little Sister

My brother dreams of being a hero one day.

A super one, he likes to say.

A big help in the time of need,

Patrolling the city, doing good deeds.

He dreams of lending a helping hand,

Protecting boys and girls, defending the land.

Making people feel safe, and defeating what's bad,

Creating much happiness for those who are sad.

I know he will be great at it, you see,

He does a great job, protecting me.

My sister dreams of being a princess one day.

A royal one, she likes to say.

A powerful companion when there's the need,

Planning noble parties, doing good deeds.

She dreams of lending a helping hand,

Protecting boys and girls, defending the land.

Making people feel happy, and defeating what's bad,

Causing much joy to those who are sad.

I know she will be great at it, you see,

She does a great job watching over me.

Daddy

Only with dad, can I pretend to drive a racecar.

I can ride my bike fast, and go really far.

I can soar like an airplane,

Play cops and robbers in the rain,

And he helps me collect slimy bugs in a jar.

Dad protects me, and always keeps me safe.

In the mornings before school, he makes sure I'm awake.

He gives me candy before I eat,

Sometimes he lets me sit in his special seat.

Dad takes me to school if I'm late.

My daddy is a friend 'til the end.

Whenever we race, he lets me win.

He tells the best stories,

Teaches me not to worry,

And whenever I need a hand, he's there to lend.

Dancing in the Sun

I am a princess. I am a princess-ballerina-butterfly.

I twirl to the beat of my drum,

Circling high into the sky.

Rum. Pum. Pum. Pum.

There is no limit to where I soar.

The rhythm guides me to places I've never seen before.

Cotton Candy Clouds and Lollipop Trees,

Soaring high, surrounding me.

The wind ruffling my hair, and the sun beams my face,

Moves me higher and higher to this beautiful place.

Visions of purple leotards and pink tutus,

Make me blissful and powerful,

I make my own rules.

I am a princess, a princess-ballerina-butterfly.

When I dance I am happy.

I am radiant when I am free.

My chasse takes the lead.

All eyes are on me!

Dream Big

Dream big, little girl,

Don't settle for less.

You can be anything you want to be,

And you can be the best.

An accountant, a professor, a ballet dancer, or an author

Whatever your heart desires for,

Work hard and you will capture.

A gymnast, a baker, a model, or a blogger

Just keep on pushing and prepare for success, beautiful daughter.

Dream big, little boy,

Reach for the stars.

The world is at your fingertips, it's not very far.

A doctor, a soccer player, a professor, or a wrestler.

You can do it. I have faith in you.

You can do anything you desire to do.

The President, a CEO, a musician, or a magician

Be confident, stand tall, and know your wealth.

You were made for greatness. Believe in yourself.

These are my hopes for you, that in everything you do,

Be the best you can be, be happy,

And I will be happy too.

First Day of School

Agghh!! I feel sick today.

My tummy feels weird.

I cannot play.

My throat is dry, my hands are wet.

My legs are shaky.

I have the flu, I'd bet.

I think I want to stay home instead,

And work on my dance moves, or just stay in bed.

My dad says, "It's just the first day jitters."

First day jitters? Oh, that sounds bad!

I may need to see a doctor, and get some meds,

Chuck down some soup and rest my head.

Just one more day will do,

And I'll be ready, I'll be brand new.

Just another day, and I'm sure I'll be ready,

Ready for my first day, ready for school.

Good Night, Sleep Tight

Good night, sleep tight.

I'll see you in the morning light.

Before I'm all tucked in bed,

There's a few things to do, then I can rest my head.

Brushing my teeth keeps them clean and bright.

I won't get cavities if I do it just right.

A super silly bedtime story helps me to relax, it seems.

The stories make me happy and cheerful, and give me sweet dreams.

Next it's time to pray to God and thank him for my friends,

My family, dogs, and cat, and for forgiving my sins.

Right before the light is off, I take another look around,

To make sure all my buddys are near, to keep me safe and sound.

There's Oscar, there's Ryan, Stuffy, and Piggy too.

They're waiting on me to snuggle in, and I know just what to do.

I kiss mom good night, as she turns off the light,

Close my eyes tight until she's out of sight.

The house is quiet, the night is sound.

All is still, all is found.

Good night Mommy, good night Daddy.

Good night Sissy, good night Teddy

Good night, sleep tight, I'll see you in the morning light.

Mommy

I love my mommy a bunch.

She sends me yummy treats for lunch.

She loves me for me,

As far as I can see,

And she makes the best pancakes for brunch.

Mommy laughs at all of my jokes.

Then, she likes to share them with folks.

She wipes away my tears,

And calms all my fears.

She even makes an awesome French toast.

My mom gives the best back rubs.

She fills my bath water with suds.

She takes care of me,

Always has a bandage for my knee.

She gives super high fives and hugs.

New Friends

Sometimes I feel a little scared,

Other times I'm shy.

Most of the time I just don't know what to say, when I'm the new guy.

Will they like me? Will they think I'm funny, cool, and fast?

Will they think I'll be a good friend in their class?

Should I ask for their names, or what's their favorite food?

"It's not easy," I tell myself. They may not be in the mood.

"Just be yourself," I can hear Dad say. "They'll love you; they have to!"

But when I try to be myself, I start to trip over my shoe.

My palms get sweaty, my knees start to shake.

It's hard to make new friends, for heaven's sake!

What if they don't think I'm creative, nice, or smart?

What if they make fun of me? That would break my heart.

I closed my eyes and took a deep breath,

Walked very slowly, and turned to the left.

What is your name?

Can I play in the next game?

I made three friends that one day at school.

They all think I'm smart, funny, fast and cool.

We love to play together, laugh and pretend.

Yep, I did it. I made three best friends.

Out to Play

Mom said I should go out to play.

She says I've been inside enough today.

"It's too nice to be indoors."

"There's a lot to see, and too much to explore."

"Ok," I thought. "I'll give it shot."

I'll put down my game, that I love a lot,

And head out to play on this sunny Saturday.

Before I knew it, I was a gold medalist of the 50 yard dash.

I was a world known superhero, protecting people,

Lending help in a flash.

I was a police officer, a veterinarian,

A football player, and a Mayor!

I was a bounty hunter, a farmer,

A business man, and a barber.

The choices were mine to be whatever I wanted,

With no limitations, and no disappointments.

All because on one fun day,

My mom suggested I go out to play.

Pet Parent

I never knew at seven years old, I would have a dog who loves me.

I never thought I would have so much responsibility.

I walk my puppy in the rain, in the sleet and snow.

I like to take him wherever I go.

Whenever he is around, he brightens up my day.

He makes me happy, and I don't know how.

He always finds a way.

We like to play fetch, and work on tricks.

I cheer him on and he gives me lots of licks.

We go on long walks, and we play soccer together.

We roll in the mud. We are best friends forever.

When I'm away at school, my puppy is sad all day.

He waits for me to come home to play.

I make sure he has water, treats, and yummy food.

Sometimes we watch TV together, if I'm in the mood.

My puppy is the best pet baby, as far as I can see.

I rescued him, but he actually rescued me.

Summer Break

No going to bed on time.

No single file lines.

No worksheets.

No assigned seats.

No alarm clocks.

No clean socks.

No cafeteria food.

No going to school when I'm not in the mood.

No getting dressed if I do not want to.

No spelling tests out of the blue.

No tardies.

No. classroom. Birthday. Parties.

No field trips.

No monkey bar grips.

No lunchtime fun.

No Field Day in the sun.

No P.E. relay races.

No story time silly faces.

No seeing my friends every day.

No calling teams when we go outside to play.

No school for three whole months, that's true.

Oh, what am I going to do?

The Library Visit

I used to think libraries were not fun or cool.

I thought it was just a place with too many rules.

You have to be quiet, walk slowly, and whisper.

It's no place for excitement, or playing tag with your sister.

Until I found out, what was there to explore,

The places you can go, all the open doors.

Through books you can become a zappy Zombie Hunter,

Go on massive adventures, move mountains in a slumber.

You can pretend to be a dancing dinosaur, a fire spitting dragon,

A big snorty pig, or a squeaky red wagon.

At a library visit, I can choose to be me, or not me at all.

I can be a creature, both big and small.

I can be any thing, and anything at all.

I'd love to be a fruit tree, so yummy and sweet,

Or a jumping bean named Ben, whom you would love to meet.

The library is by far, my most favorite place.

It makes me happy, and puts a smile on my face.

Today I chose to be a barging blue hippo.

What I'll choose tomorrow, I'm sure no one knows.

The Worst Day of my Life

If there was ever a worst day, that day was today,

The day I got grounded,

And my toys went away.

They were gone without warning,

Disappeared without trace.

What was once there was no more,

Like they all were erased.

What's a kid to do,

When his day turns to poo?

This was the worst day of my life, so I just stared at my shoe.

"Think about your actions."

"Work on your reactions."

I've learned my lesson, I could say.

But would that matter anyway?

I chose to sat still, and watch the time click away,

Wishing I could go out to play.

It felt like forever, this horrible day!

That's when I heard a knock on my door,

And just like that, my punishment was no more.

I hugged my parents, and kissed them goodnight.

I hoped somehow they'd forget about my big fight.

32

Made in the USA
Columbia, SC
27 June 2018